SPOT 50
Space

Sue Becklake

First published in 2012 by Miles Kelly Publishing Ltd
Harding's Barn, Bardfield End Green, Thaxted, Essex, CM6 3PX, UK

2 4 6 8 10 9 7 5 3 1

Publishing Director Belinda Gallagher

Creative Director Jo Cowan

Editorial Assistant Lauren White

Designer Kayleigh Allen

Production Manager Elizabeth Collins

Reprographics Stephan Davis, Thom Allaway

ISBN 978-1-84810-584-3

Printed in China

British Library Cataloguing-in-Publication Data
A catalogue record for this book is available from the British Library

ACKNOWLEDGEMENTS
All artworks are from the Miles Kelly Archives

The publishers would like to thank the following sources for the use of their photographs:
Key: t = top, b = bottom, c = centre, l = left, r = right

Dreamstime.com 1; 49 **Fotolia.com** 4(tl), (tr) Stephen Coburn
iStockphoto.com 15 Jan Rysavy; 25 Jim Mills; 50 Shaun Lowe
NASA 9 Robert Gendler; 51 Dominic Cantin
NASA Goddard Space Flight Center (NASA-GSFC) 32
NASA Headquarters – Greatest Images of NASA (NASA-HQ-GRIN) 30
NASA Jet Propulsion Laboratory (NASA-JPL) 6; 14; 28; 33; 37
NASA Marshall Space Flight Center (NASA-MSFC) 27; 39
Shutterstock.com 4(br) Terrance Emerson; 25 Muellek Josef; 31 William Attard McCarthy
Science Photo Library 5 Frank Zullo; 24 Tony & Daphne Hallas **Phil Cowan** 4(bl)

Every effort has been made to acknowledge the source and copyright holder of each picture.
Miles kelly Publishing apologies for any unintentional errors or omissions.

Made with paper from a sustainable forest

www.mileskelly.net info@mileskelly.net
www.factsforprojects.com

CONTENTS

Tick the circles when you have spotted the space objects.

HOW TO WATCH THE NIGHT SKY

You can spot some of the fascinating things in space, such as planets, moons and stars, just by looking for them in the night sky. Others are too far away to see without a powerful telescope but there are many pictures of these in library books and on the Internet.

When and where to watch the night sky

Choose a dark, clear night when there are no clouds and the Moon is not shining. Pick a dark spot, away from houses and street lights, with a clear view of the sky. In cities, the lights swamp out fainter stars but the Moon and the brighter stars are still visible. Gradually you will be able to see more stars as your eyes adapt to the dark.

Binoculars and telescopes

Binoculars and telescopes make distant objects look brighter and nearer. They show many more stars, detail on the Moon, and the shapes of nebulae and distant galaxies. Telescopes are often more powerful than binoculars but reveal a smaller patch of sky.

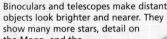

Maps of the night sky

Astronomers use maps called star charts to find their way around the night sky. They show star patterns called constellations, with the larger dots marking the brighter stars. A planisphere is a star chart that shows which stars are visible at different times throughout the year.

How to find the planets

Although most planets shine brighter than stars, they are difficult to find as they move across the constellations. Magazines and websites give details on when and where to see the planets. Only five are bright enough to be seen with the naked eye. The brightest is Venus, seen here next the Moon.

HOW TO STUDY THE SUN SAFELY

WARNING: Never look at the Sun especially with binoculars or a telescope. Sunlight can seriously damage your eyes or even make you blind.

You cannot study the Sun by looking at it directly, but you can safely look at an image of it made with a telescope. Always ask an adult to help you do this.

Making an image with a telescope

You need a small telescope and two sheets of white cardboard. Cut a hole in one sheet to fit over the telescope eyepiece. Point the telescope towards the Sun without looking through it or through the finder scope – keep a lens cap on the finder scope. Put the other card in the shadow of the first. Tilt the telescope until you can see an image of the Sun on this screen.

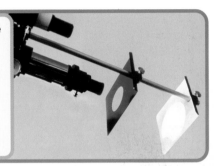

Pinhole viewer

If you don't have a telescope you can make a small image of the Sun with two pieces of cardboard. Make a small hole using a large pin in the first piece of card. Then hold it facing the Sun with the other piece of card behind it so the shadow of the first card falls on the second card. Start with the cards close together and look for a small, bright spot of light, the image of the Sun. If you move the cards further apart the spot will get bigger but less bright.

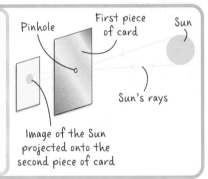

Pinhole

First piece of card

Sun

Sun's rays

Image of the Sun projected onto the second piece of card

HOW TO SPOT SYMBOLS

Look for pictures in books or on the Internet

Look in the daytime sky (naked eye)

Look with binoculars or a telescope

Look in the night sky (naked eye)

Only look at a projected image

THE SUN.

The Sun is a star, but it looks bigger than all the other stars because it is much nearer. It is a huge ball of extremely hot gases. In the centre it is so hot that the gases fuse together, making energy. It gives out this energy as light and heat – without this nothing could live on the Earth. The Sun is surrounded by a family called the Solar System. It includes the Earth, seven other planets, moons, comets and asteroids, all circling the Sun.

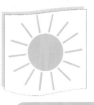

SEE WITH

Explosions on the Sun called solar flares look like huge flames or loops of hot gas shooting out from the surface.

FACT FILE

Diameter of Sun 1,392,530 km
109 times Earth's diameter
Mass of Sun 330,000 times Earth's mass
Distance from Earth
149.6 million km
Spins Once every 25 days at Equator

Solar flare

Solar prominence is a gigantic arc of hot hydrogen

WARNING: Never look at the Sun especially with binoculars or a telescope. Sunlight can seriously damage your eyes or even make you blind.

SUNSPOTS

If you project an image of the Sun using binoculars or a telescope, you may be able to see some dark spots. These are called sunspots. They are slightly cooler than the rest of the Sun, but they are still extremely hot. Look again on the next sunny day and you will see that the sunspots have moved. This is because the Sun rotates over a period of 28 days. The number of spots on the Sun varies, with a peak every 11 years.

SEE WITH

No sunspots were seen for 70 years between 1645–1715. This time was called the Little Ice Age – the winters on Earth were very cold and the river Thames in London froze.

FACT FILE

Average temperature of sunspot 4000°C

Temperature of Sun's surface 5500°C

Size of smallest sunspots About 300 km across

Size of largest sunspots About ten times Earth's diameter

Sunspots usually appear in pairs or groups

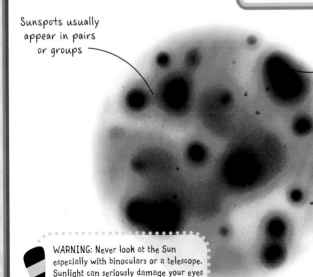

Some large sunspots last for months

Small, individual sunspots may only last for a few days

WARNING: Never look at the Sun especially with binoculars or a telescope. Sunlight can seriously damage your eyes or even make you blind.

SOLAR ECLIPSE

Sometimes the Sun, Moon and Earth all line up so that the Moon is directly in front of the Sun. The Moon blocks out the sunlight, causing its shadow, only a few kilometres wide, to fall on the Earth. This is called an eclipse of the Sun. If you are in the shadow you will see a total eclipse – the Sun completely disappears for a few minutes. Just outside the shadow you will see the Moon covering part of the Sun – this is a partial eclipse.

SEE WITH

The Sun and Moon appear to be the same size. But the Sun is 400 times larger than the Moon, and 400 times further away.

DATES

FUTURE TOTAL SOLAR ECLIPSES

When	Where
13 Nov 2012	Australia, N. Zealand, S. Pacific, S. America
3 Nov 2013	Eastern Americas, S. Europe, Africa
20 Mar 2015	Iceland, Europe, N. Africa, N. Asia
9 Mar 2016	E. Asia, Australia, Pacific
21 Aug 2017	N. & S. America
2 July 2019	S. Pacific, S. America

The Sun's corona, a ring of white glowing gas, is only seen during an eclipse

The Moon completely covers the Sun in a total eclipse

THE MOON

Most of the planets have moons circling around them. The Earth's Moon is one of the largest in the Solar System. It is a round ball of rock smaller than the Earth, and it is very dry and dusty with no air or water. We see it shining brightly in the sky because it reflects light from the Sun. Look for a Full Moon rising in the east just after the Sun has gone down. A New Moon appears in the west in the early evening, but soon disappears below the horizon.

SEE WITH

Over three billion years ago another planet probably crashed into the Earth, throwing rock out into space to make the Moon.

FACT FILE

Diameter 3476 km
27% Earth's diameter

Mass 1.2% Earth's mass

Distance from Earth 384,400 km

Time for one orbit of Earth
27.3 days

Spins Once in 27.3 days

Dark areas are low, flat plains called seas

Craters made by space rocks crashing into the Moon's surface

PHASES OF THE MOON

Watch the Moon for a month and you will see it appear to change shape from a **Full Moon to a thin, crescent shape.** These are the phases of the Moon. It does not actually change shape – as it circles the Earth we only see the part that is lit by the Sun. When the whole of the sunlit side faces the Earth there is a Full Moon. When the sunlit side is facing away from Earth, we cannot see it at all and there is a New Moon.

SEE WITH

People used to believe that a Full Moon could send some people mad. The word 'lunatic' comes from the Latin word 'luna', meaning Moon.

OBSERVATION

WHEN TO LOOK FOR
New Moon (first visible crescent)
After sunset
First Quarter Moon Afternoon
and early night
Full Moon Sunset to sunrise (all night)
Last Quarter Moon Late night
and morning

③ Half Moon

④ Gibbous Moon

② Crescent Moon

⑧ During the second half, the Moon wanes (dwindles) back to a crescent-shaped Old Moon

⑤ Full Moon

① New Moon

⑥ Gibbous Moon

⑨ Crescent Moon

⑦ Half Moon

LUNAR ECLIPSE

An eclipse of the Moon happens when the Sun, Earth and Moon are lined up. The Moon passes through the Earth's shadow as it orbits the Earth. If the whole Moon goes into the shadow there is a total eclipse. If only part of the Moon goes into the shadow there is a partial eclipse. An eclipse of the Moon can only happen when there is a Full Moon and can last for over an hour. It can be seen from anywhere on Earth where it is night time.

SEE WITH

There is not an eclipse every time there is a Full Moon because the Moon's orbit is tilted. Mostly, the Moon goes above or below the Earth's shadow, not through it.

DATES

FUTURE TOTAL LUNAR ECLIPSES
15 April 2014
8 October 2014
4 April 2015
28 September 2015
31 January 2018
27 July 2018
26 May 2021
16 May 2022
8 November 2022

THE CHANGING APPEARANCE OF THE MOON AT DIFFERENT STAGES DURING AN ECLIPSE

① ② ③ ④ ⑤

① The Moon moves into the Earth's shadow at the start of an eclipse
② Partial eclipse with most of the Moon in shadow
③ Total eclipse
④ Moving out of the shadow
⑤ Eclipse almost ended

11

MOON CRATERS & SEAS

The Moon is covered in round scars called craters. These were made billions of years ago by space rocks crashing onto the surface. With binoculars you can see the larger craters – some are hundreds of kilometres wide. The best time to look is when there is a Half Moon. You can also see dark and light patches on the Moon. The darker parts are low, flat plains. People used to think these were oceans and called them 'seas' – we now know they are completely dry.

SEE WITH

The Moon spins at the same time that it orbits the Earth, so we can never see the far side of it from Earth.

FACT FILE

DIAMETERS OF SOME CRATERS

Archimedes 82 km

Tycho 102 km

Copernicus 107 km

Plato 109 km

Ptolemy 164 km

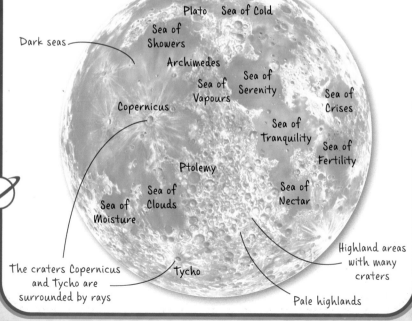

Plato   Sea of Cold

Sea of Showers

Dark seas

Archimedes

Sea of Vapours

Sea of Serenity

Sea of Crises

Copernicus

Sea of Tranquility

Sea of Fertility

Ptolemy

Sea of Moisture

Sea of Clouds

Sea of Nectar

The craters Copernicus and Tycho are surrounded by rays

Tycho

Highland areas with many craters

Pale highlands

MERCURY

The closest planet to the Sun, Mercury is also the smallest planet. It is very hot because it is so close to the Sun, with temperatures reaching 430°C during the day. At night, the side that faces away from the Sun gets colder than the lowest temperatures on Earth, reaching as low as −180°C. Mercury is difficult to spot in the sky because it is so close to the Sun. Look for it just after sunset, near the horizon where the Sun has set, or just before sunrise.

SEE WITH

Mercury's day is twice as long as its year. It spins once in nearly 59 days, but the time from one sunrise to the next is 176 days because it orbits the Sun in only 88 days.

FACT FILE

Diameter 4879 km, 38% of Earth's diameter

Mass 5.5% of Earth's mass

Distance from Sun 57.9 million km

Time for one orbit (year) 88 days

Spins Once in 58.6 days

Surface temperature −180° to 430°C

The largest crater, called the Caloris Basin, is 1550 km wide and 2 km deep

WARNING: Never look at Mercury with binoculars or a telescope — it is too close to the Sun.

Mercury is deeply dented with craters made by space debris crashing into it

VENUS

The second planet from the Sun is Venus. It is about the same size as Earth and is covered with thick clouds. Venus is the brightest object in the night sky apart from the Moon. It is often called the Evening or Morning Star because it shines brightly in the western sky soon after sunset, or in the eastern sky just before dawn. Venus has phases like the Moon – with binoculars you may see a crescent shape.

SEE WITH

Surface clouds trap heat, making Venus hotter than an oven. Venus' atmosphere presses down 90 times harder than the air on Earth.

FACT FILE

Diameter 12,104 km, 95% of Earth's diameter
Mass 82% of Earth's mass
Distance from Sun 108.2 million km
Time for one orbit (year) 225 days
Spins Once in 243 days
Surface temperature 465°C

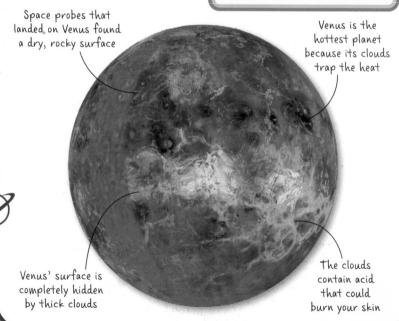

Space probes that landed on Venus found a dry, rocky surface

Venus is the hottest planet because its clouds trap the heat

Venus' surface is completely hidden by thick clouds

The clouds contain acid that could burn your skin

EARTH

The planet we live on is a huge ball of rock whirling through space. Earth is the third planet from the Sun and the largest of the four rocky planets in the Solar System. Satellite photos show a round, blue planet surrounded by a thin layer of air with white clouds. Two-thirds of its surface is covered with oceans and seas. It is the only planet we know of that has water on the surface and an atmosphere that living creatures can breathe.

SEE WITH

The Earth is teeming with all kinds of living things – plants, animals, insects, microbes – but scientists have not found life anywhere else in the Solar System.

FACT FILE

Diameter 12,756 km
Mass 5.97 x 1024 kg (1024 means million million million million)
Distance from Sun 149.6 million km
Time for one orbit (year) 362.5 days
Spins Once in 23.9 hours
Surface temperature −89° to 58°C

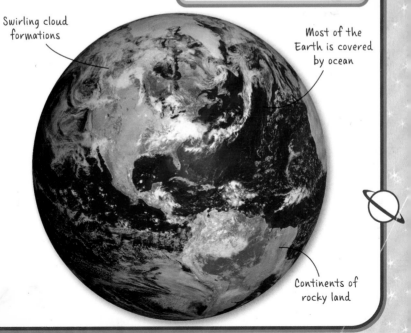

Swirling cloud formations

Most of the Earth is covered by ocean

Continents of rocky land

MARS

Like Mercury, Venus and Earth, Mars is a small, rocky planet. It is the fourth planet from the Sun. Mars is smaller than Earth and colder because it is further from the Sun. It is often called the red planet because the rocks and dust on its surface are rusty red in colour, however it has white ice caps like the Earth. In the sky, Mars looks like a bright star with a reddish colour, but to see any detail you will need a telescope.

SEE WITH

Mars has the largest volcano in the Solar System. Olympus Mons is nearly three times higher than Mount Everest. Luckily it is probably extinct and won't erupt.

FACT FILE

Diameter 6794 km, 53% of Earth's diameter
Mass 11% of Earth's mass
Distance from Sun 227.9 million km
Time for one orbit (year) 687 days
Spins Once in 24.6 hours
Surface temperature −130° to 30°C

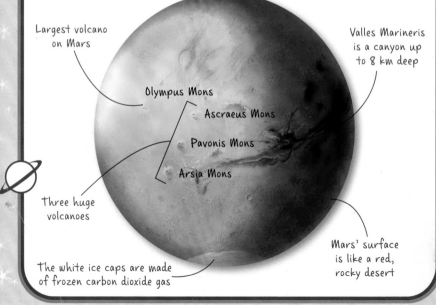

Largest volcano on Mars

Olympus Mons

Ascraeus Mons

Pavonis Mons

Arsia Mons

Valles Marineris is a canyon up to 8 km deep

Three huge volcanoes

Mars' surface is like a red, rocky desert

The white ice caps are made of frozen carbon dioxide gas

JUPITER

Jupiter's mass is larger than all the other planets put together. It is the largest planet in the Solar System and fifth planet from the Sun. Jupiter is called a gas giant because it is made of gas and liquid, with a small rocky core hidden deep in the middle. It looks like a bright white star in the sky. With binoculars you can spot its four largest moons as dots on either side of the planet. They change places as they move around Jupiter.

SEE WITH

Jupiter spins so fast that it bulges out around the middle. Its speedy spin makes the colourful clouds stretch out into orange-and-yellow bands around the planet.

FACT FILE

Diameter 142,984 km,
11.2 times Earth's diameter
Mass 318 times Earth's mass
Distance from Sun 778.3 million km
Time for one orbit (year) 11.86 years
Spins Once in 9.9 hours
Surface temperature −140°C

Fierce winds swirl Jupiter's clouds into oval storms

Light stripes are called zones

Bands of different-coloured clouds stretch around Jupiter

The Great Red Spot is a huge whirling storm larger than the Earth

Dark stripes are called belts

SATURN

Another gas giant planet, Saturn is almost as large as Jupiter but nearly twice as far from the Sun. It is the sixth planet from the Sun. Saturn's clouds are not as bright as Jupiter's, but it makes up for this with its spectacular rings, which stretch out in a disc around its Equator (an imaginary line around the centre of the planet). Saturn looks like a bright yellow star in the sky. It is the faintest of the planets you can see with the naked eye, but you will need a telescope to see its rings.

SEE WITH

Saturn's rings shine brilliantly because they are made of billions of small, icy chunks all orbiting the planet. Some are as small as an ice cube and others the size of a car.

FACT FILE

Diameter 120,536 km, 9.45 times Earth's diameter
Mass 95 times Earth's mass
Distance from Sun 1433 million km
Time for one orbit (year) 29.66 years
Spins Once in 10.65 hours
Surface temperature −180°C

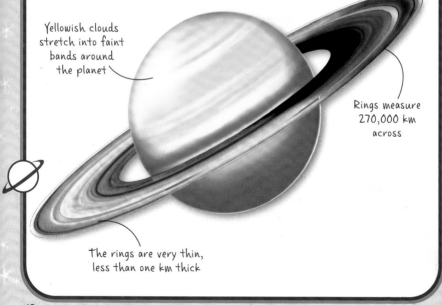

Yellowish clouds stretch into faint bands around the planet

Rings measure 270,000 km across

The rings are very thin, less than one km thick

URANUS

Uranus is the seventh planet from the Sun. It is made of gas and icy materials, and is covered with clouds, giving it a blue-green colour. It is so far away that it is very difficult to see in the sky without a telescope. The Voyager 2 space probe sent back close up pictures of the planet and its larger moons when it flew past in 1986. Pictures taken by the Hubble Space Telescope just show a few bands of cloud and occasionally a dark storm.

SEE WITH

Uranus is barely visible from Earth. It looks like a very faint star with the naked eye, and was not identified until 1781 by William Herschel.

FACT FILE

Diameter 51,118 km
4 times Earth's diameter
Mass 14.5 times Earth's mass
Distance from Sun 2873 million km
Time for one orbit (year) 84 years
Spins Once in 17.24 hours
Surface temperature −1950°C

Uranus tilts so far on its side it seem to roll around the Sun

Green-blue methane clouds surround the planet

Rings of ice and dust surround the planet

NEPTUNE

Neptune is made of gas and ice like Uranus, but it is a little smaller and its clouds look **blue.** It is the coldest planet because it is furthest from the Sun's warmth. It cannot be seen without a telescope. Pictures taken by the Voyager 2 space probe, which flew past the planet in 1989, show white wispy clouds and a dark storm patch. When the Hubble Space Telescope looked at Neptune in 1996 this storm had disappeared.

SEE WITH

Neptune has the fastest winds in the Solar System. They blow around its Equator at over 2000 km/h, five times faster than the strongest winds on Earth.

FACT FILE

Diameter 49,528 km
3.9 times Earth's diameter
Mass 17.15 times Earth's mass
Distance from Sun 4495 million km
Time for one orbit (year) 165 years
Spins Once in 17.24 hours
Surface temperature −2000°C

Faint ring system

Storm patch called the Great Dark Spot

DWARF PLANETS

Dwarf planets are much smaller than the **eight main planets.** The five named so far are all smaller than the Moon. They are round balls made of rock, or rock and ice. The nearest to the Sun, Ceres, orbits the Sun between Mars and Jupiter. Pluto is beyond Neptune and even further away are Haumea, Makemake and Eris. None of the dwarf planets can be seen without a telescope, and even with the largest telescopes the furthest three look like stars.

SEE WITH

Pluto was discovered in 1930 and became the ninth planet after Neptune. It was demoted in 2006 when astronomers started to find other dwarf planets.

FACT FILE

DIAMETERS OF THE DWARF PLANETS (in order of distance from The Sun)
Ceres 975 km
Pluto 2306 km
Haumea 1150 km
Makemake 1500 km
Eris 2340 km

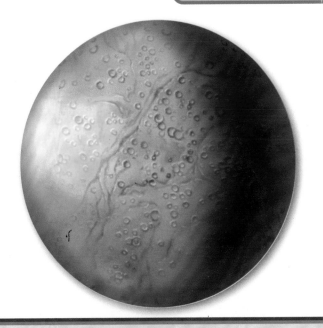

ASTEROIDS

Sometimes called minor planets, asteroids are chunks of rock of all different sizes. Most circle the Sun in the asteroid belt between Mars and Jupiter. The largest, Ceres, is now called a dwarf planet, but there are millions of smaller ones, many only the size of large boulders. Astronomers keep a look out for any that might come close enough to Earth to hit us. You need a telescope to spot even the largest asteroids, but spacecraft have sent back some pictures.

SEE WITH

A Japanese space probe called Hayabusa (falcon) landed on the asteroid Itokawa, collected some dust and brought it back to Earth for scientists to study.

FACT FILE

DIAMETERS OF LARGEST ASTEROIDS

Ceres 952 km

Pallas 544 km

Vesta 529 km

Hygeia 431 km

A mix of small and large rocks make up the asteroid belt

COMETS

Often described as dirty snowballs, comets are small chunks made of ice and dust. They are usually too small and far away to be seen, even by powerful telescopes. When a comet comes close to the Sun, the ice melts, forming a giant, glowing tail of gas and dust. This is what we see in the sky. Some comets reappear, such as Halley's Comet, which orbits the Sun every 76 years. Others turn up unexpectedly. It is rare to see a bright comet with the naked eye.

SEE WITH

Halley's comet is named after Edmund Halley (1656–1742). He predicted that it would return in 1758. It was the first time a comet's arrival had been predicted.

FACT FILE

Typical size of nucleus 1–10 km
Typical length of tail Up to 150 million km
TYPES OF COMET
Periodic Take less than 200 years to orbit the Sun
Long period Take longer than 200 years for one orbit

Tail points away from the Sun

Tiny nucleus hidden inside cloud of glowing gas

Huge glowing tail of gas and dust thousands of kilometres long

METEOR SHOWERS

Shooting stars are not stars at all. They are streaks of light, made by small bits of dust or rock from space hitting the Earth's atmosphere. They move so fast that they burn up in the air. The streak lasts for only a few seconds and is called a meteor. The best time to look for meteors is during a meteor shower when there may be one every few minutes. Meteor showers happen when the Earth travels through a trail of dust left behind a comet.

SEE WITH

During a meteor shower, all the meteors seem to come from the same place. Each shower is named after the constellation the meteors seem to come from.

DATES

METEOR SHOWERS HAPPEN ON THESE DATES EVERY YEAR

Name	Date	Constellation
Quadrantids	3–4 Jan	Boötes
Perseids	23 Jul–20 Aug	Perseus
Orionids	16–31 Oct	Orion
Leonids	15–20 Nov	Leo
Geminids	7–16 Dec	Gemini

① A meteor causes a quick flash of light

② In a meteor shower, meteors may appear as often as one every minute

③ Some meteors are brighter than others

④ Meteors usually appear one at a time, but a photo taken during a shower can show many together

METEOROIDS & METEORITES

Pieces of rock and dust racing around the Sun in space are called meteoroids. They range in size from tiny specks of dust to large rocks. Meteoroids hit the Earth all the time, but most burn up in the Earth's atmosphere. Only the biggest fall to the ground and these are called meteorites. It is very rare to see a meteorite falling or even on the ground, so look for displays of them in museums.

SEE WITH

The largest meteorite was found in Namibia, in Africa. It is called the Hoba meteorite and weighs about 60 tonnes. This meteorite still lies where it was found in 1920.

FACT FILE

TYPES OF METEORITE

Stony Made mostly of rock
Iron Made mostly of iron mixed with another metal called nickel
Stony-iron A mixture of rock and iron
Mars/Moon Rock that has been chipped off the Moon or Mars

Smooth, shiny surface was melted when the meteorite heated up as it plunged into Earth's atmosphere

IRON
METEORITE

CHONDRITE (STONY)
METEORITE

Most meteorites found on Earth are stony meteorites

STARS

Stars are huge glowing balls of very hot gas. On dark, clear nights you should be able to see up to about 2000 stars without a telescope, but only about 100 are bright enough to be spotted easily. Some stars really are large and bright, but others look bright because they are closer to us. The stars make patterns in the sky called constellations. You can use constellations to find your way around the night sky.

SEE WITH

Sirius, the brightest star in the sky, is also called the 'Dog Star'. It has a much smaller, fainter companion star nicknamed 'The Pup'.

LOOK FOR

THE FIVE BRIGHTEST STARS IN SKY

Name	Constellation	Where visible
Sirius	Canis Major	N&S
Canopus	Carina	S
Arcturus	Boötes	N
Alpha Centaurus	Centaurus	S
Vega	Lyra	N

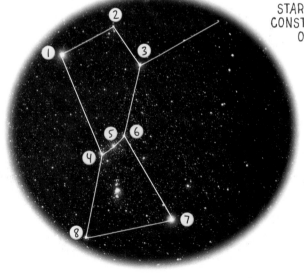

STARS OF THE CONSTELLATION ORION

1. Betelgeuse
2. Meissa
3. Bellatrix
4. Alnitak
5. Alnilam
6. Mintaka
7. Rigel
8. Saiph

GIANT & DWARF STARS

Stars vary enormously in size and temperature. The Sun is a medium-sized star and looks yellow in colour. Larger, hotter stars look bluish, and small, cool stars look red. At the end of their lives, stars like the Sun swell up into red giant stars, becoming much larger and cooler. In billions of years the Sun will get large enough to swallow up the nearest planets. Eventually a tiny white dwarf star will be all that is left of the Sun.

SEE WITH

The largest star that astronomers have found is called the R136a1. They think it is 265 times larger than the Sun and ten million times as bright.

LOOK FOR

DIFFERENT-COLOURED STARS

Colour	Name	Constellation
Blue-white	Rigel	Orion
White	Vega	Lyra
Yellow-white	Capella	Auriga
Orange	Arcturus	Boötes
Red	Antare	Scorpius

PISTOL NEBULA

Blue hypergiant, the Pistol Star is hidden by dust

Clouds of dust and gas

STAR CLUSTERS

Unlike the Sun, most stars have companions, usually two or more stars circling around each other. Larger groups of stars are called clusters. Huge groups of thousands or millions of older stars are called globular clusters due to their ball shape. Open clusters are smaller groups of young stars that have formed close together. Some open clusters can be seen with the naked eye, but a telescope is needed to see most globular clusters.

SEE WITH

LOOK FOR

CLUSTERS

Name	Type	Constellation	
Pleiades	Open cluster	Taurus	N
Beehive	Open cluster	Cancer	N
Jewel Box	Open cluster	Crux	S
Omega Centauri	Globular cluster	Centaurus	S

The Pleiades star cluster is known as the Seven Sisters – although most people can pick out only six stars of the hundreds in the cluster.

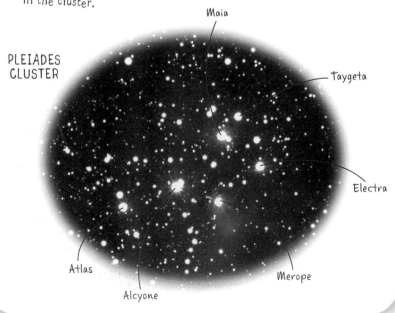

PLEIADES CLUSTER

Maia

Taygeta

Electra

Merope

Alcyone

Atlas

BRIGHT NEBULAE

A nebula (plural nebulae) is a cloud of dust and gas between stars. Most of the gas and dust in space is invisible. We only see it if light from a nearby star makes the gas glow. Stars are born in these clouds when clumps of gas and dust collapse into balls. These shrink, getting smaller and hotter until they shine as stars, making the surrounding gas glow as a bright nebula. They look like fuzzy patches in the sky, but telescopes show their colours and detail.

SEE WITH

Dying stars leave clouds of dust and gas, which eventually become the nebulae where new stars and planets form.

LOOK FOR

BRIGHT NEBULAE
Orion Nebula
Lagoon Nebula
Rosette Nebula
Eagle Nebula
Tarantula Nebula
Trifid Nebula

Clouds of dust heated by young stars

TRIFID NEBULA

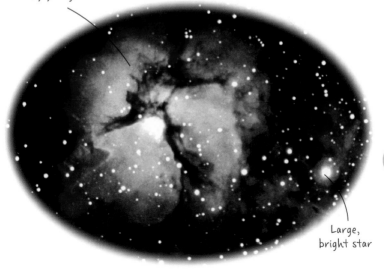

Large, bright star

REFLECTING NEBULAE

We see some nebulae not because the gas glows, but because the dust reflects light from nearby stars. These reflecting nebulae look blue because the dust grains reflect more blue light than red light. They often look like a blue haze around or near a star. Pictures of the Pleiades star cluster taken with a telescope show a faint blue haze around the stars. This is because the stars are moving through a dusty part of space.

SEE WITH

Hubble's Variable Nebula is a strange reflecting nebula that appears to change its shape. This may be due to shadows cast by moving patches of dust.

LOOK FOR

REFLECTING NEBULAE
Boomerang Nebula
Witch Head Nebula
Hubble's variable Nebula
NGC 1977 and M78 in Orion
Pleiades

NGC 1977
REFLECTING NEBULA

Dust grains reflect more blue light than red

DARK NEBULAE

Some dusty nebulae do not glow or reflect
light, but we can see them because they
**block out light from stars or bright nebulae
behind them.** These are called dark
nebulae. Some look like dark holes in the
sky where there are no stars. Others look
like dark patches in bright nebulae. Stars form
in these dark, cool clouds. When light from new
stars makes the surrounding gas cloud glow, we
see the dark nebula silhouetted
against a glowing nebula.

SEE WITH

Most of the dark clouds of dust
and gas in space are invisible.
Astronomers use radio telescopes
to find out where they are.

LOOK FOR

DARK NEBULAE
Coalsack
Cone nebula
Horsehead nebula
Pillars in Eagle nebula

HORSEHEAD
NEBULA

Dark, swirling clouds
of dust and gas make
a horsehead shape

PLANETARY NEBULAE

A planetary nebula is a shell of gas around a dying star. They all have their own unique shapes and colours. At the end of its life an ordinary star swells up to become a red giant star, and its outer layers expand out into space. For thousands of years, light from the remaining star makes the gas glow as a planetary nebula then it fades, leaving a tiny white dwarf star. Giant stars end their lives in an explosion called a supernova, which throws out a glowing nebula called a supernova remnant.

SEE WITH

Planetary nebulae have nothing to do with planets. Early astronomers just thought they looked like round planets through their small telescopes.

LOOK FOR

PLANETARY NEBULAE
Helix Nebula
Ring Nebula
Eskimo Nebula
Eight-burst Nebula
Cat's Eye Nebula
Crab Nebula – supernova remnant

EIGHT–BURST NEBULA

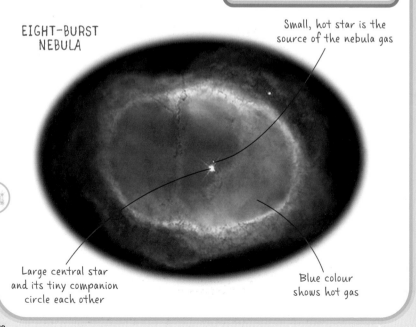

Small, hot star is the source of the nebula gas

Large central star and its tiny companion circle each other

Blue colour shows hot gas

SPIRAL GALAXIES

Galaxies are huge families of stars. There are billions of galaxies out in space and each contains many millions or even billions of stars. Some are called spiral galaxies because of their shape. They have a bulge of stars in the middle and spiral arms curling outwards from the bulge in a flat disc shape. You can see a few galaxies without a telescope, but these look like fuzzy patches. Large telescopes show the beautiful spiral patterns.

SEE WITH

LOOK FOR

SPIRAL GALAXIES
Andromeda Galaxy M31
Triangulum Galaxy M33
Whirlpool Galaxy M51
M100
M101
NGC 1300 – barred spiral Galaxy

Barred spiral galaxies have a bar across the centre instead of a bulge, with arms curling out from the ends of the bar.

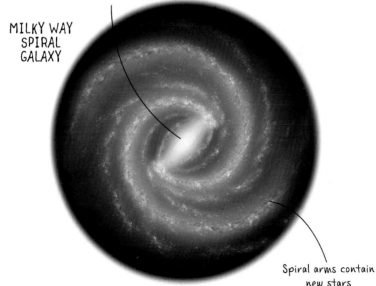

Central bulge
contains old stars

MILKY WAY
SPIRAL
GALAXY

Spiral arms contain
new stars

ANDROMEDA GALAXY

The most distant object you can see with the naked eye is the Andromeda Galaxy. Find it from the W shape of Cassiopeia. Follow a line between its centre-right stars (1), down to a large square with a star at each corner – the constellation Pegasus. Follow another line from the bottom-right corner of the square (2), back towards Cassiopeia. The Andromeda Galaxy is a fuzzy patch two-thirds of the way along. Binoculars show its oval shape and bright centre.

SEE WITH

The Andromeda Galaxy is on a collision course with the Milky Way. Billions of years from now they may pull each other apart and form a new, giant galaxy.

FACT FILE

BEST TIME TO LOOK
October–February

Distance 2.3 million light years

Diameter 150,000 light years

The Andromeda Galaxy can be seen from the Northern Hemisphere.

PEGASUS

ANDROMEDA GALAXY

CASSIOPEIA

ANDROMEDA

MILKY WAY GALAXY

We cannot see the Milky Way's spiral shape because we are inside the galaxy. The Sun is in one of the arms about two-thirds of the way out from the centre. The Milky Way looks like a very faint uneven band of light across the sky. You can see it on very clear, dark nights, and with binoculars you will be able to see separate stars. Look for it in the southern constellations of Sagittarius and Scorpius in the winter and in the northern constellation of Cygnus in the summer.

SEE WITH

FACT FILE

Diameter 100,000 light years
Number of stars 200 billion
Distance of Sun from centre 25,000 light years
Shape Large spiral

Stars circle the centre of the Milky Way, and the Sun takes 226 million years to make one orbit, called a galactic or cosmic year.

CRUX

CYGNUS

MILKY WAY

MILKY WAY

SCORPIUS

CASSIOPEIA

SAGITTARIUS

SOUTHERN HEMISPHERE

NORTHERN HEMISPHERE

ELLIPTICAL GALAXIES

Not all galaxies have a spiral shape. Elliptical galaxies are shaped like a huge squashed ball. Some are quite small with only a few million stars, but many are giants with billions of stars. Most of the stars in elliptical galaxies are old and there are no clouds of dust and gas where new stars can form. Some giant elliptical galaxies may have been formed when two spiral galaxies collided. They can grow by gobbling up other galaxies that get too close.

SEE WITH

Giant elliptical galaxies are often in the centre of large clusters of galaxies that are close enough to collide into each other.

LOOK FOR

ELLIPTICAL GALAXIES

M87

M32

NGC 1132

NGC 4881

ESO 325-G004

Fuzzy shape with little dust or stars

NGC 1132
ELLIPTICAL GALAXY

Blue colour indicates the presence of hot gas

IRREGULAR GALAXIES

Some galaxies do not have a definite shape. These are called irregular galaxies and are usually smaller than the other types of galaxy with fewer stars. Many irregular galaxies contain plenty of gas and dust clouds where new stars can form. Astronomers call these starburst galaxies. Our Milky Way Galaxy has two small irregular galaxies as companions called the Magellanic Clouds. These are visible with the naked eye from the Southern Hemisphere.

SEE WITH

Both the Magellanic Clouds are circling our Milky Way Galaxy and will eventually be torn apart and pulled into it.

LOOK FOR

IRREGULAR GALAXIES
Large Magellanic Cloud
Small Magellanic Cloud
NGC 4490
NGC 1427A
IC 1613

No definite shape to galaxy, lots of dust and gas

IC 1613
IRREGULAR
GALAXY

SOUTHERN HEMISPHERE GALAXIES

The Large and Small Magellanic clouds are the nearest galaxies to the Milky Way. They look like cloudy patches in the sky. A line across the corner of Crux (1) leads to the Large Magellanic Cloud, which is mostly within the constellation Dorado. Look at it with binoculars to see brighter patches, which are nebulae or star clusters. A line down the length of Crux (2) points to the Small Magellanic Cloud, within the constellation Tucana.

SEE WITH

The Large and Small Magellanic clouds were named after the Portuguese explorer Ferdinand Magellan, who spotted them in 1521, nearly 500 years ago.

DORADO

LARGE MAGELLANIC
CLOUD

CRUX

SMALL MAGELLANIC
CLOUD

TUCANA

COLLIDING GALAXIES

Galaxies sometimes get so close to one another that they collide. They do not bounce off each other because they mostly contain empty space between the stars. They may pull each other out of shape, forming tails of gas and dust. Sometimes they merge together into one larger galaxy. Some giant galaxies swallow up smaller nearby galaxies. New stars often form where the gas and dust is swept into thick clouds by these collisions.

SEE WITH

The Milky Way and Andromeda spiral galaxies are moving towards each other and will probably collide in about five billion years time.

LOOK FOR

COLLIDING GALAXIES
The Mice – NGC 4676
Antennae Galaxies – NGC 4038 and 4039
Tadpole Galaxy – ARP 188
ARP 271
ARP 272

THE MICE. COLLIDING .GALAXIES

Long tail of hot gas

Spiral galaxy

Spiral galaxy

NORTHERN HEMISPHERE

The Plough is a group of seven bright stars within the constellation Ursa Major. The seven stars form a saucepan shape. The two stars at the bottom of the Plough are called the Pointers. They lead to Polaris, the Pole Star, which marks the North Celestial Pole. Follow a line from the Plough (1), past Polaris (2), to find the W shape of the constellation Cassiopeia. Look left along the 'handle' of the Plough (3) to an orange star, Arcturus, the brightest star north of the Equator.

SEE WITH

The second star from the end of the Plough's handle, Mizar, is a double star with another star called Alcor. You may be able to see them both with the naked eye.

OBSERVATION

BEST TIMES TO LOOK
Ursa Major February–May
Ursa Minor May–June
Cassiopeia October–December
Boötes May–June

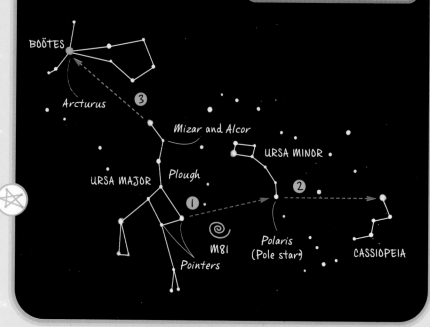

BOÖTES

Arcturus

③

Mizar and Alcor

URSA MINOR

URSA MAJOR Plough

①

②

M81

Pointers

Polaris (Pole star)

CASSIOPEIA

SOUTHERN HEMISPHERE

Four bright stars in the shape of a small cross make up the constellation Crux. An imaginary line along its length (1) points to the South Celestial Pole, although there is no bright pole star. Two bright stars close to Crux are the Southern Pointers. They are the brightest stars in the constellation Centaurus. Follow a line from the Pointers (2), across the bottom of Crux, to the constellation Carina. Its brightest star is Canopus – the second brightest star in the sky.

SEE WITH

Alpha Centauri is really a group of three stars. One of these, Proxima Centauri, is the nearest star to the Sun, but you cannot see it with the naked eye.

OBSERVATION

BEST TIMES TO LOOK
Crux April–May
Centaurus April–June
Carina January–April

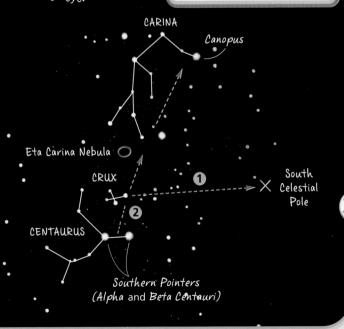

CARINA

Canopus

Eta Carina Nebula

CRUX

South Celestial Pole

CENTAURUS

Southern Pointers
(Alpha and Beta Centauri)

ORION

The constitution Orion is one of the most recognizable. Orion was a great hunter in Greek mythology. A line of three bright stars make up the hunter's belt. Below the belt is a smaller line of stars, the hunter's sword, with the fuzzy patch of the Orion Nebula in the middle. Binoculars show the shape of the nebula with its newborn stars. Two giant stars mark Orion's foot and shoulder – Betelgeuse is an old red giant (1) and Rigel is a younger blue giant (2).

SEE WITH

OBSERVATION

BEST TIME TO LOOK
December–January
Can be seen from the Northern and Southern hemispheres.
If you live in the Southern Hemisphere, the pattern will appear upside down – the sword will be above the belt, Rigel will be at the top left and Betelgeuse will be at the bottom right.

Betelgeuse is about 500 times larger than the Sun and about 14,000 times brighter. If it replaced the Sun, it would swallow up all the planets to Mars, including Earth.

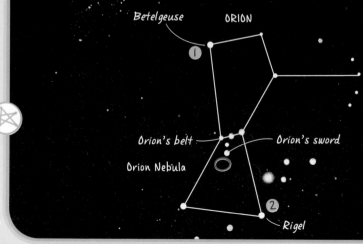

Betelgeuse

ORION

Orion's belt

Orion's sword

Orion Nebula

Rigel

BRIGHT STARS NEAR ORION

Sirius, in the constellation Canis Major, is the **brightest star in the sky.** Follow a line from Orion's belt (1), down to the left, to find Sirius. A line from Rigel (2), through the middle of Orion's belt, takes you up to the constellation Gemini. Its two brightest stars are Castor and Pollux. Moving left across Orion's shoulders from Betelgeuse (3), you can see the bright star Procyon, in the constellation Canis Minor. It makes a bright triangle in the winter sky with Betelgeuse and Sirius.

SEE WITH

Castor looks like one bright star, but telescopes show a group of three stars. Each of these is also a double star, so Castor is actually a double double double star.

OBSERVATION

BEST TIME TO LOOK
Canis Major January–February
Gemini January–February
Canis Minor February
Can be seen from the Northern and Southern hemispheres.
If you live in the Southern Hemisphere, the patterns will appear upside down.

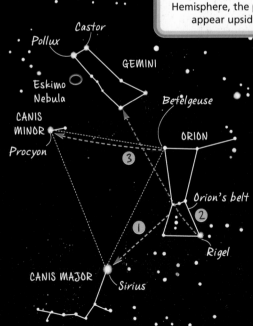

TAURUS

Aldebaran, an old red giant star, marks the eye of the bull, Taurus. Follow a line up from Orion's belt (1) to find Aldebaran. Close to it is a V-shaped cluster of stars called the Hyades. You can see these clearly with the naked eye, but binoculars show even more stars. Follow the same line (2) to come to another bright cluster of young stars called the Pleiades. Look for about six stars with the naked eye and many more with binoculars.

SEE WITH

The Crab Nebula, in the constellation Taurus, is the remains of an exploding star. Chinese astronomers saw the explosion nearly 1000 years ago in 1054.

OBSERVATION

BEST TIME TO LOOK

Taurus December–January

Can be seen from the Northern and Southern hemispheres.

If you live in the Southern Hemisphere, the patterns will appear upside down.

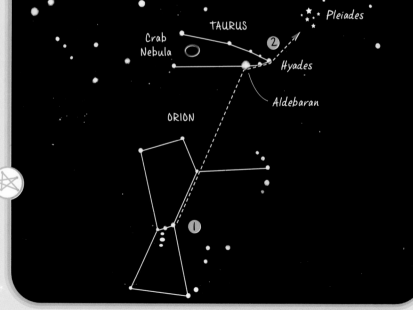

Pleiades

TAURUS

Crab Nebula

② Hyades

Aldebaran

ORION

①

SUMMER TRIANGLE

In the Northern Hemisphere summer sky, three bright stars mark the corners of the Summer Triangle. They are all from different constellations. The brightest star in the triangle is Vega (1), in the constellation Lyra. Altair is in the constellation Aquila (2) and Deneb is in the constellation Cygnus (3). Lyra and Aquila are not very bright, but you can see the swan shape of Cygnus. Deneb is the swan's tail. Its neck stretches to the middle of the Summer Triangle, with the wings on either side.

SEE WITH

In 10,000 years time, the Earth will have tilted so that Vega will be nearer to the North Celestial Pole than Polaris is. It will become the pole star.

OBSERVATION

BEST TIME TO LOOK

Lyra July–August

Aquila July–August

Cygnus August–September

The Summer Triangle is seen in the Northern Hemisphere in summer.

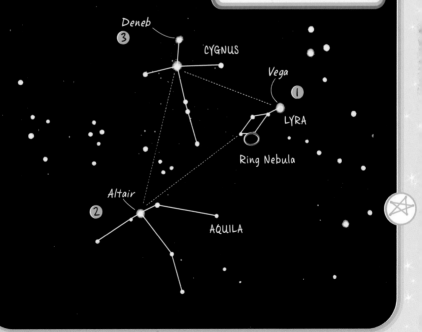

Deneb
③

CYGNUS

Vega

①

LYRA

Ring Nebula

Altair
②

AQUILA

SCORPIUS

In the Southern Hemisphere sky, the constellation Scorpius is easy to recognize because it looks like a scorpion with a curled tail. Find it along a line from Crux, through the Southern Pointers (1). The bright red star in the middle of Scorpius, Antares, is a red supergiant star. Near the tail (2) is the teapot shape of the constellation Sagittarius. Look for the Lagoon Nebula near the lid of the teapot. You can just see it with the naked eye, but binoculars give a better view.

When you look at Sagittarius, you are looking towards the centre of our Milky Way Galaxy. The centre is hidden behind clouds of dust in the spiral arms of the galaxy.

OBSERVATION

BEST TIME TO LOOK

Scorpius June–July

Sagittarius July–August

These constellations can be seen from the Southern Hemisphere.

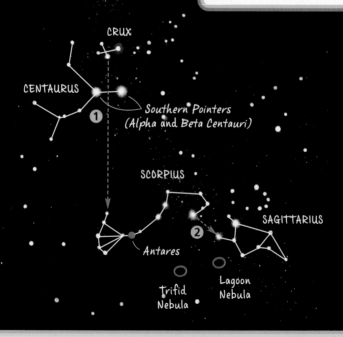

CRUX

CENTAURUS

① Southern Pointers
(Alpha and Beta Centauri)

SCORPIUS

SAGITTARIUS

②

Antares

Trifid
Nebula

Lagoon
Nebula

LEO

The constellation Leo looks a little like its name, a crouching lion. Its head is made of a group of six stars that look like a backwards question mark called the Sickle. You can find Leo from the Plough. Follow a line through the Plough's Pointers in the opposite direction to the Pole Star to find the Sickle. The brightest star in Leo, called Regulus, is the bottom star of the Sickle. It marks the lion's front leg while another bright star, Denebola is at the end of its tail.

SEE WITH

Every November there is a meteor shower in Leo called the Leonids. Every 33 years the shower becomes a storm with many more shooting stars.

OBSERVATION

BEST TIME TO LOOK

March–April

Northern and Southern hemispheres

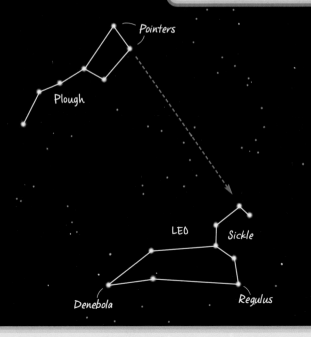

Pointers

Plough

LEO

Sickle

Denebola

Regulus

CENTAURUS

Centaurus is a constellation in the southern skies. You can find it wrapped around Crux, the Southern Cross. Its two brightest stars, Alpha and Beta Centauri, are easy to spot. Alpha Centauri is the fourth brightest star in the sky and the nearest star system to us. There is also another smaller red star in the group called Omega Centauri, which looks fuzzy with the naked eye. Telescopes show that it is a globular cluster of stars – the largest and brightest in the sky.

SEE WITH

In ancient Greek myths a Centaur was a beast with the head and chest of a man and the body and legs of a horse.

OBSERVATION

BEST TIME TO LOOK
April–June
Southern Hemisphere

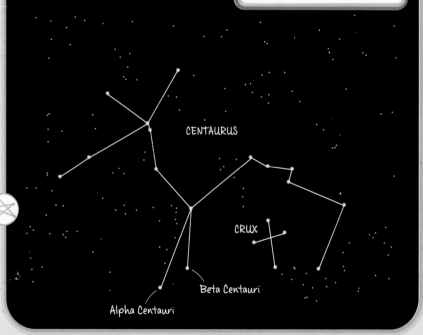

CENTAURUS

CRUX

Beta Centauri

Alpha Centauri

NORTHERN & SOUTHERN LIGHTS

The Northern and Southern lights (auroras) are glowing lights in the sky near the North or South poles. They happen when tiny atomic particles from the Sun plunge into the Earth's atmosphere, making the gases in the air glow. You can usually only see them from areas in the far North, such as Norway or Alaska, or in the far South, such as Antarctica. They look like moving green or red lights across the sky.

SEE WITH

The Northern and Southern lights are brightest every 11 years, when there are the most sunspots on the Sun. This should happen again in 2013.

FACT FILE

Height of Aurora At least 100 km

Colours Green or red – glowing oxygen
Pink or blue – glowing nitrogen

Shapes Arc – curved glow
Band – like a ribbon
Ray – vertical lines

Names Aurora Borealis – Northern Lights
Aurora Australis – Southern Lights

Shimmering green glow of the Northern Lights

Dark sky above the forest trees

HALOS & SUNDOGS

The air around the Earth often causes strange lights in the sky. A halo is a ring of light around the Moon or the Sun. This happens when they shine through a thin cloud made of ice crystals. The crystals bend some of the light, making a ring appear. Look for a halo around the Moon when it is full, or nearly full. Sundogs are patches of light like mini rainbows on either side of the Sun. They are also made by ice in the air. You can sometimes see moondogs on either side of the Moon.

SEE WITH

The ice crystals that make halos and sundogs have six sides and they form in clouds 5–10 km up in the atmosphere.

FACT FILE

Distance between Sun or Moon and halo, sundog or moondog 22° – about the width of two fists at arms length

Maximum height of sundogs in the sky 60° – two-thirds of the way from the horizon to overhead

① ② ③ ④

WARNING: Look for sundogs when the Sun is fairly low in the sky with thin clouds. Do not look at the Sun itself – block it out with your hand.

① Setting Sun
② Halo
③ Sundog
④ Sundog

SATELLITES

You can often see man-made satellites or the International Space Station orbiting Earth. They look like a slow-moving bright star. If you see one with flashing lights it is probably an aeroplane, not a satellite. Look for them soon after sunset when the sky is getting dark, but the satellite is still lit by the Sun. Iridium satellites spin around and make a bright flash as they reflect sunlight. These flashes are called iridium flares.

SEE WITH

The International Space Station takes only 1.5 hours to circle Earth. It travels through space at a speed of about 28,000 km/h, nearly 30 times faster than a jumbo jet.

FACT FILE

ORBITS OF THE INTERNATIONAL SPACE STATION AND IRIDIUM SATELLITES

	ISS	Iridium
Height (km)	350	780
Time for one orbit of Earth (min.)	91	100
Number of orbits per day	15.7	14.4

Trail made by the International Space Station as it crosses the sky

FLYBY SPACE PROBE

Astronomers send space probes to take a closer look at the planets and moons in our Solar System. These probes collect information to send it back to Earth. Some fly past, while others go into orbit or land on a planet. Flyby space probes, Voyagers 1 and 2, both visited Jupiter and Saturn, then Voyager 2 went on to fly past Uranus and Neptune also. They sent back close-up pictures of the planets and their moons.

SEE WITH

The two Voyager probes are now speeding out of the Solar System. Voyager 1 is the most distant spacecraft at over 17 billion km from the Sun.

TIMELINE

	Voyager 1	**Voyager 2**
Launch	September 1977	August 1977
Jupiter	March 1979	July 1979
Saturn	November 1980	August 1981
Uranus		January 1986
Neptune		August 1989

Cameras

Magnetometer boom to detect magnetic fields

VOYAGER 2

Radioisotope generators

Main antenna received commands from Earth and sent back information as radio signals

Antennae to pick up radio waves

ORBITING SPACE PROBE

Mercury, Venus, Mars, Jupiter and Saturn have all been explored by orbiting space probes. These can map whole planets and spot events such as erupting volcanoes. The Cassini probe arrived at Saturn in 2004. It carried a smaller probe called Huygens that landed on Saturn's largest moon Titan. The main Cassini probe continues to orbit Saturn. It has mapped the surface of Titan, which is hidden by clouds, and found icy jets and possible underground water on Enceladus, another of Saturn's moons.

SEE WITH

Cassini has found rivers, lakes, rain, snow, mountains and maybe volcanoes hidden beneath Titan's hazy clouds.

FACT FILE

Launched 15 October, 1977

Arrived Saturn 30 June, 2004

Distance travelled
3.5 billion km

Size 6.7 m high x 4 m wide

Main antenna

Magnetometer to measure Saturn's magnetism

Disk-shaped Huygens lander bolted to Cassini's side

Radar bay

CASSINI

Generator

MARS ROVERS

Of the many space probes that have landed, the Mars Exploration rovers are **exceptionally successful.** Two robots called Spirit and Opportunity landed at different places on Mars. They crawled across the surface on their six wheels testing the soil, taking pictures and using their drills to explore the rocks. They found that in the past there was probably water on the surface of Mars, but now it is very dry.

SEE WITH

FACT FILE

	Spirit	Opportunity
Launched	10 June	7 July, 2003
Landed on Mars	4 January	25 January, 2004
Distance travelled	8 km (approx.)	19 km (approx.)

Size Height 1.5 m, width 2.3 m, length 1.6 m

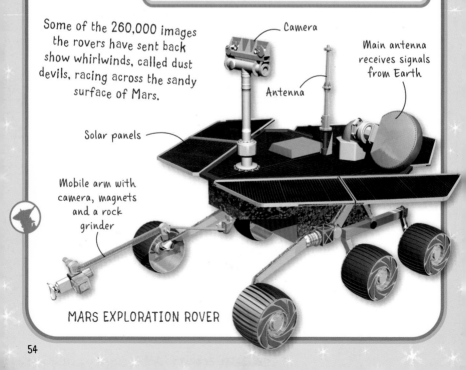

Some of the 260,000 images the rovers have sent back show whirlwinds, called dust devils, racing across the sandy surface of Mars.

Camera

Main antenna receives signals from Earth

Antenna

Solar panels

Mobile arm with camera, magnets and a rock grinder

MARS EXPLORATION ROVER

ASTRONOMY SATELLITES

Telescopes above the atmosphere have a clearer view of distant space. They also collect radiation that cannot get through the atmosphere, so can tell astronomers about events such as exploding stars. The Hubble Space Telescope has been orbiting the Earth for over 20 years. Like telescopes on Earth it has a mirror to collect light and make images. These show glowing nebulae, and galaxies so far away that their light has taken billions of years to reach us.

SEE WITH

Shuttle astronauts have flown five servicing missions to the Hubble. Each time they replaced some of its instruments with better ones, giving an even clearer view of space.

FACT FILE

Launch 24 April, 1990 by space shuttle Discovery
Size 13.2 m long, 4.2 m diameter
Mirror diameter 2.4 m
Orbits the Earth in 97 minutes
Travels at 28,000 km/h

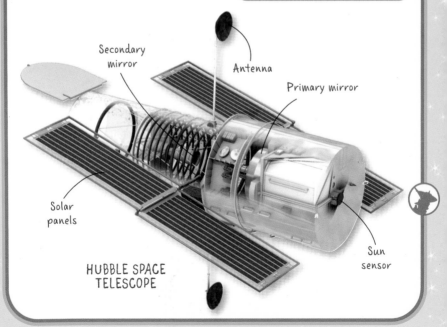

Secondary mirror

Antenna

Primary mirror

Solar panels

Sun sensor

HUBBLE SPACE TELESCOPE

GLOSSARY

Asteroids Lumps of rock orbiting the Sun mostly between Mars and Jupiter.

Atmosphere The layer of gas around a planet, moon or star, such as the air around the Earth.

Aurora (Northern and Southern lights) The display of moving coloured lights in the sky near the North or South poles.

Comet A lump of rock and ice that forms a huge glowing tail when it gets close to the Sun.

Constellation A pattern made by the stars in the sky.

Dwarf planet Round ball of rock or ice orbiting the Sun but smaller than the main planets.

Eclipse When an object, e.g. the Moon, moves in front of another object, e.g. the Sun, and hides it.

Galaxy A huge group of millions or billions of stars.

Hemisphere A half of the Earth, divided by the Equator. The Northern Hemisphere is north of the Equator and the Southern Hemisphere south of the Equator.

Light Year The distance that light travels in one year. The speed of light is about 300,000 km per second. One light year is 9.5 million million kms.

Meteor A streak of light made by a rock from space burning up as it plunges into the Earth's atmosphere.

Meteorite A space rock that lands on Earth.

Meteoroid A piece of rock or dust racing around the Sun in space.

Nebula A cloud of dust and gas in space, only seen when the gas glows or dust blocks out light from behind it.

Orbit The path of one object, such as a moon, around another object, such as a planet.

Planet A large rocky or gassy ball that orbits a star.

Radio telescope A telescope that collects radio waves instead of light to make images.

Satellite Anything that orbits a larger object. Moons are natural satellites. Man-made satellites are called artificial satellites.

Solar System The family of planets, moons and smaller objects that orbit the Sun.

Space probe A robot spacecraft that travels to space and sends images and information back to earth.

Star A huge ball of hot gas that gives out heat and light e.g the Sun.

Star chart A map of the night sky.

Sunspots Dark patches on the Sun that are slightly cooler than the rest of the Sun's surface.

Supernova An enormous explosion that blows apart giant stars at the end of their lives.

Variable stars Stars that do not shine steadily and appear to change in brightness.